Bitter Creek Junction

Other works by Linda M. Hasselstrom:

Feels Like Far (The Lyons Press)
Bison: Monarch of the Plains (Graphic Arts Center Publishing)
Land Circle (Fulcrum, Inc.)
Going Over East (Fulcrum, Inc.)
The Roadside History of South Dakota (Mountain Press)
Dakota Bones (Spoon River Poetry Press)
Windbreak (Barn Owl Books)
Journal of a Mountain Man: James Clyman, editor (Tamarack Books)
Leaning into the Wind, co-editor (Houghton Mifflin)

Bitter Creek Junction

Linda M. Hasselstrom

POETRY OF THE AMERICAN WEST SERIES

HIGH PLAINS PRESS

Printed in the United States of America.

Jacket photograph © Pro-Visions 2000

FIRST PRINTING

1 3 5 7 9 8 6 4 2

Many of these poems are for Jerry, of course. But the book is also for the women who shared my Windbreak House Retreat during the summer of 1999 as I revised these poems—women who turn the crossroads, bumps and potholes of our journey into poetry.

Library of Congress cataloging in publication data

Hasselstrom, Linda M.
Bitter Creek Junction / Linda M. Hasselstrom.
p.cm.--(Poetry of the American West)
ISBN 0-931271-53-3 (trade paper)
1. Ranch life--West (U.S.)--Poetry. 2. Women--West (U.S.)--Poetry.
I. Title. II, Series.

PS3558.A7257 B58 1999
811'.54 21--dc21

99-043718

HIGH PLAINS PRESS
539 CASSA ROAD
GLENDO, WY 82213
1-800-552-7819
CATALOG AVAILABLE

CONTENTS

WHERE THE STORIES COME FROM

JIGSAW DANCE

BITTER CREEK JUNCTION

WHERE THE STORIES COME FROM

Make a Hand

"Make a hand!" my father hollered when my friends came down to visit.
Almost everyone I knew would come to help us, just so they
could nod when conversations turned to ranching. "Make a hand!" He didn't
care if they were men or women when we needed help. "This job's
beyond an old man and a crippled girl," he'd say. "Make a hand
and drive those yearlings up the chute so we can take 'em to the sale.
Your mother wants new carpet but I think I'll get a truck." Gender
issues didn't surface, not until we got around to branding.
Even then he didn't call them that. He'd just yell, "Make a hand,"
and startle a romantic poet who'd never had a callus, who spent
his nights consulting with his muse, a scribbler whose idea of work
was sitting by a candle sighing while he doodled at his latest
masterpiece, a villanelle on spring and love. "Make a hand!"
That skinny poet vaulted over an eight-foot plank fence when he heard it.

The writer grabbed a calf's tail—frozen short the night his mother
birthed him, March and forty-two below. An artist slammed the headgate,
flipped the calf and held him while I laid a red hot iron
against his ribs. Before that calf discovered his potential he had
lost them both; was branded, ear tagged, and received his shots, and lurched
away. The poet headed back to get another critter, jeans
still oozing with authentic green manure as Dad yelled "Make a hand!"
It's been six years or better since we closed the box, that narrow casket
where he finally took his rest. We tamped the yellow gumbo down
that summer, filled and tamped some more come spring. I planted wild blue flax,
brought plugs of redtop from the pasture, big and little bluestem. Found
a sego lily like the ones he brought my mother every spring.
The gumweed flourished, creeping jenny, thistles. When I yanked them out
barehanded, I could hear him mutter that I should be wearing gloves.

"Make a hand!" I hear him shout when I quit work and wander out
to see if I've got mail today. "Make a hand!" he bellers when
I sit to read a bit of some new book before I start our lunch.
"Make a hand!" he hollers when I'm waking or asleep. He treated
me no different than the son he never had. He scrimped and saved
and criticized until the day he died, dropping dead outside
the kitchen door the way he always said he wanted to.
He left the ranch to mother, even though she hated it and had
no man to help her. I got nothing, but I helped her sort the mess
he left, found money in the rafters, deeds stuffed inside a garbage
can beneath the cellar steps. I put her money in a trust
so she could have the care she needs in that new nursing home in town.
I added up the debts and stood beside his grave and cussed him hard.
I took a deep breath, got a loan and bought the ranch. And every time
I step outside, I hear the echoes, "Make a hand!" ∽

The Cost of a Badger Hat

Last night I dreamed of you,
face intent, peeling grizzled hide
from a badger you once shot to make a hat.
I remember how you shot
then swore, wishing you had not,
recall the way the badger hissed
and clawed your boot
before his eyes grew dim, then closed.
You tanned the hide:
stitched the eyelids shut,
cut and shaped the pelt
to let the front paws dangle—
too lifelike, and too limp.
You wore it once, then packed it in your trunk.
Ten years next moonrise since I buried you.
Every time I cleaned the house, I shoved
the trunk a little farther back
beneath the stairs.

This summer's solstice woke me
with a downpour on the roof.
The sun rose in a rainbow.
Drinking coffee, I recalled
how carefully you bore the badger's bones
and flesh to that far ridge
I see each morning, left them
to the care of sun and wind.

I brought the badger hat into the light,
took it up the ridge and found a hole
some other badger hollowed out
to hunt for moles. Digging deeper,
I heard chorus frogs and ducks,
redwing blackbirds singing on their nests
among the cattails in the pond below.
I laid the badger down with gifts
of sage, sweetgrass, tobacco.
Scooped damp sand and gravel over him
and topped it with a heavy stone.

As I watched the light sink into dusk
this longest day of summer,
nighthawks skimmed the grass.
I'll smile in summer nights to come
when I will lie in bed and listen
to anxious frogs, leaping to escape
another badger prowling by the water.
I know another year
has circled toward its end,
know the land leans into darkness,
tilts toward death. And now I know
I'll dream you smiling, long hair blowing,
hatless in a sunset breeze. ☙

Haystack: May Afternoon

This great gold mound beams heat
I can't resist. My eyes drift closed.
I breathe the winter's bright chill winds
driving snow between the stems,
the musk of mice and moles
burrowing and building deep below.
A sour odor tells of cows that grazed
and fertilized this ground all winter,
lying warm to chew their cud
while ice defined their eyelashes.
I scent the doe leading her fawn
into the willows when I roared into this field
last June towing the mower.

I can almost taste the blood
that spurted when I struck
the second fawn I didn't see
until he lurched away to die alone.
A trace of July's tangy sweat
lingers in my nose, the reek
of lightning from the rumbling cloud
that rose in hues of green and black
to batter me with hail. A whiff of vapor
from the tractor fuel mingles
with hydraulic oil that leaked while
my father built this stack.

I dream
I smell the pipe the hunter smoked
while he leaned against this stack
deciding that he'd missed,
that he had no need to trail the deer
he'd stalked and shot at. He was wrong.
My husband found her, broken leg mud-caked,
drowning in the creek. He pulled her out
to hold her while she gasped and died.
Her eyes droop closed again just as I wake
within a sharp bouquet of song
a meadowlark is pouring
to tumble down the slanting hay
to where I lie. ೞ

Death of the Last Cowhand

For Hobie Morris, after all this time

I'm pretty sure Tom Blasingame
was dressed at sunrise that December morning
on the Texas plains. Sipped
his coffee hot while Eleanor made breakfast.
Finished off a second cup,
pecked her on the cheek and pulled his hat
down tight. He saddled up the colt,
a three-year-old, and raised a hand as he
rode off. Likely she was watching
from the kitchen window. He headed out
toward Palo Duro Canyon, thinking
how he'd stayed there at the Campbell Creek Camp
nine miles south all week when he
first married Eleanor. She settled down
in town until he got a house
fixed at the ranch.
He figured he could check
the windmill, teach the colt his manners.
Be sure that sucker rod was holding firm.
The bay colt snorted once or twice,
crow-hopped and mouthed the bit, but nothing out
of line. The sun shone warm on Tom's
lean back but he stayed cagey, minding how
the colt's ears flickered back and forth.
He may have smiled a little, thinking back
to other horses, a lot of other nags.
At ninety-one, he couldn't count
them all but he'd been working on that ranch
nearly sixty years, breaking
horses, chasing cows, doing work
he loved. Hadn't left the place
since he came back from Arizona, nineteen
and thirty-four.

The JA hands
found him just past sunset, stretched out
on the prairie grass, boots on,
hat across his face. The horse stood guard.
Old Tom had not one scratch or bruise.
The hands who found him figured he'd be proud
he wasn't pitched. "Must have known
he was in trouble," said the cattle foreman.
One man headed back to take
the word to Eleanor while the others brought
him in. I wonder if they did
it right, slung him over his own saddle
for his last trip home. Or went
and got a pickup. Later Eleanor told
a newsman she had never seen
a bunch of cowboys cry before. They all
sat with her on the porch recalling
Tom, and how he pulled his weight right up
until the end. Every one
agreed that Tom had won the hand, gone out
the way he wanted. A cowboy all
his life, Tom knew, they figured, when he saw
the Horseman coming, who he was.
He would have recognized the silhouette—
the hood he wears, no proper hat.
He'd see the great sharp scythe, and know the horse—
may have rode him years ago.
Know the bay colt couldn't run as fast.
Still, he took his time, dismounting
so he wouldn't scare the colt. Dropped
the reins in case the bay ran off.
He may have met the Horseman on his feet, or lay
down on the sod he never had
to plow. They couldn't tell. But either way,
Tom Blasingame has died the way
he lived and all of us have cause to miss him. ☙

Making Chokecherry Jam

Two grandmothers—Jerry's
and my own—join me in our kitchen
this November night, although they both
died years ago and never met.

Cora tilts her head down
peering at the jars in boiling water,
smiles her blessing on me.
Mary sits down, sighs,
picks up the Sure Jell box,
looks at it and shakes her head.

Cora eyes the plastic padding
on my new jar lifter. I can
almost hear her say, "My stars!
What will they think of next?"

As she sits by Mary, I see
the mottled burn scar on her arm
and recall her telling me
how once she dropped a pot
of scalded jars and boiling water
as she moved it from the old
wood-burning stove.

Last time I tried to make
chokecherry jelly, it didn't stiffen.
Jerry said chokecherry syrup
is better anyway, made pancakes
more often that winter. I'd like to ask
these two old experts for their secrets.
But for me to speak might drive
these fragile shades away.

I startle when the phone rings,
flinging crimson droplets on the floor.
My aunt, still very much alive, has called
to comment on how frail my mother's grown,
how well they treat her in the nursing home.
Mother hated cooking, sent me every summer
to my grandmother's house where I absorbed
the skills I've learned to love.

I tell my aunt I'm cooking chokecherries,
ask her how much Sure Jell I should add
to make the jam solidify.
She sniffs and says she never bought
pectin, her tone insinuating
the young are always wasteful.
"It's the pulp that thickens jam," she says.
"Don't strain it out."

From the kitchen, I hear Mary mutter,
"Pulp. That's the secret." My aunt
goes on to say she taught her sons
to make chokecherry jam not long ago,
laughing as she adds, "I really enjoyed
being able to say, 'Hand me that spoon.'
Most of the years I spent in that kitchen,
the boys were somewhere else
and I was all alone. Guess that's one
of the benefits of getting older."

After she hangs up, I go back
to the kitchen and the smiling,
silent women I didn't mention
to my aunt. The room congeals
with memories. A ruby waterfall of jam
cascades and fills each jar.

I top all but one with heated paraffin,
watching Cora's age-stained hands—
now my own—tilt the jars to make a seal.
Mary fills the empty pot with suds,
begins to scrub as Jerry
comes into the room. I wonder how
to introduce the women, but they are gone.

"The jam is setting up," I say instead.
His verdict's "Good. Just luck?"
I seem to see light flare off
a pair of specs, detect a fading smile.
"Oh," I say, "I got some good advice
from women of experience." ☙

International Incident

On a still summer day,
the blue gelding wants
an excuse to buck.
He snaps his feet up,
sets them down
as if the dirt was glass.
At the prairie dog town,
he snorts, quivers,
seeing in every hole
a horse-eating snake.
I'm ready: legs flexed,
body balanced. He arcs
his neck, springs to the side.
I spur to bring him back,
expecting to see a rattler.
Instead, six tiny owls,
stacked one atop another
inside a burrow,
crouch and glare.
The top one spreads his wings
two whole inches, inhales,
hisses, clicks a tiny beak.
Silver down shining,
they jostle, each owl
trying to climb
just one owl higher. ೞ

Extended Forecast

For Jerry, February 14, 1996

"Stay off the roads," the forecast says.
"There's mountain snow and valley rain."
But I head home. No mountain snow,
no valley rain will stop me now.

I've loved each minute of the trip,
eating snacks and reading in bed,
watching late-night wildlife shows.
You relished silence in our empty house,
tossed your socks and boots around,
fed the dog with tidbits from your plate.
Each night you told me, "Drive careful now,
the roads are slick with mountain snow and valley rain."
Late tonight we'll eat thick steaks
and trade our tales: my meeting
with a Swedish news team in return
for your bent viaduct of steel
and stories of the crew that straightens it.

Mountain snow: the heavy flakes
stick to my windshield, crazed with cracks.
Frozen wipers clash as I pull over,
scape the ice away, and duck
as eighteen-wheelers blunder past.
I can almost smell the onions frying,
hear the swish as beer foams in my mug.
I crest the hill, fog blind, muddled
by the distances I cannot see.
Wipers hum, I grip the wheel
and plummet into valley rain.

Extended forecast: mountain snow.
My tires drone, *Don't be scared. Don't fear*
those city women. Country singers wail.
Darkness rolls down summits fleeced
in mountain snow. A downhill grade:
I'm flying through the rain that freezes
faster than my worn-out heart
or this old Ford can thaw. Momentum
boosts me up the hill. I see a cave
hollowed in sandstone where a mule deer doe
chews brush and watches mountain snow.

Topping out, I squint to see the speed sign—
seventy-five at last. I shift to overdrive,
and floor the pedal. The tires sing *do-si-do,* slip
sideways as I clutch the wheel.
Slowing down, I think of how
I hardly saw last summer's lightning
while I hummed and planted seeds,
watched thunderclouds roll up the sky.
Then thunder boomed and grumbled. Once
the skies had cleared, that other woman packed
her bags and left. *Don't be afraid,*
my tires hum now. Extended forecast:
we'll drive on together
through the mountain snow,
through valley rain. ꟹ

Walking City Streets

I walk alone on city streets at midnight.
Snow accepts my steps in silence.
Earlier, when I walked along the river,
some rooms behind the windows
flickered with blue light and sleepless people.
Now the only lights are street lamps
twinkling like the chunky snowflakes.
Strings of Christmas lights hang cold and dark,
clicking together in a rising wind.

A stained-glass window on the second floor
in back of one house tempts me.
I hunch my shoulders, turn into the alley,
pausing in the narrow space beside
a fence of planks, not really looking
at the light, only the panes of purple,
green, of gold and blue and crimson.

Behind the window, between the mellowed walls,
a woman bathes. She waited in her chair
before the fire until he pecked her
on the cheek. She waited while he climbed the stairs,
tripping over dogs. She stayed until
the mingled snores of man and dogs rolled down
the staircase. Then she stepped outside to scan
the sky and wait a little longer. Snowflakes eddied around
the street light on the corner. When her
hands grew cold, she tiptoed up the stairs,
lit the candles, snapped the light off. Filled
the tub with bubbling water, so hot she eased
in one joint at a time, breath held.

Sheltered and concealed, I close my eyes
to hear the wind cascade between the houses.
Inside the steamy room, she lies in stillness
listening as the pipes cool down, the old house
creaks and grumbles. She breathes as deeply
as she can, lingering while the water cools.
She rubs the arm still aching from her day's
work, notices his snores are slower,
tapering off. She tries to think how long
it's been since he came in to scrub her back.
When was it he last sat down on the tub's edge
to play his jaw harp while she bathed? She can't
remember. Soon she'll slide between the flannel
sheets. The older dog, his back against the man's,
will raise his head a moment while the young one
rises from the man's crooked arm to stretch.
He'll nose his way along her side until
his head is resting on her hip. They'll sigh
together, tumbling into ease.

I shake snow off my shoulders,
begin to walk the stiffness from my knees.
Another block and I can go to bed—
to watch the falling snow
until I drift to sleep. ∽

Where the Stories Come From

For Wally McRae and for Joel Nelson

"You didn't know? He died—young and hard and bad."
That voice could fill a stadium but he spoke low
and flicked a glance beneath his Stetson brim at me.
I turned away but I'd already heard enough.
The tale began to grow, to put down roots within
my brain, already thick with other tales. I chose
this job of telling stories, counting lives gone by
too soon. What I don't know, I'll guess. I suppose
his father made him tough by being cold and rugged.
He learned to be a man by never showing fear.
His mom spent all her time alone, fixing meals
and counting hours in that old ranch house
two dozen miles from town—before she met
the guitar picker she ran off with when the boy
was ten. His dad bought him a pickup when he finished
high school, took the boy to his first fancy bar.
(His sister got advice: to go to school, find
herself a husband, settle down and have some kids.)

I didn't hear enough to know if it was drugs
or drink that got this one, but I can see him gun
a graveled curve on some Montana back road,
laughing fit to kill as headlights sweep around
the bend, baffled when the stars come down to meet
him. I can hear the crash. I wonder, did he leave
some girl in terror, pregnant with the memory
of his grin? Does his dad just drink and stare
at empty spaces where he hoped for family
settled on the land that bore his name?
                                        I heard
a bit of talk I wasn't meant to hear, and now
I can't get rid of it. I might as well get dressed
and write it down. I'll sleep no more tonight. ∽

JIGSAW DANCE

A Northern Woman Takes the Golden Road

The road I take
is lined with sunflowers,
rolling south along a river gorge
and through a desert.
San Antonio Mountain guards the border.
Lightning flashes. Rain pounds his broad shoulders,
flows through his robes to steam on hot asphalt.

Chilled by autumn,
I left my home yesterday,
fleeing south before the snow clouds,
tired of locking my doors
against well-meaning friends,
tired of waiting for my dead husband
to come back.
When the phone rang in that house,
I had nothing to say.
When I started believing
the dust in the corners
was clay from his grave mound,
I flew south in search of heat and light.

Now the highway climbs
toward the canyon walls
straight ahead at La Madera.
Along the dry ravine, sand ripples like a river.
Two dogs, not on my map,
nap in the road. In an empty yard,
I stop to check my route.
Windows in crumbled adobe
are bare of curtains. A note invites, "Come in.
Shut the door when you leave."

I turn left at the post office
in the other half of the store.
The dusty street is empty.
In a garden, a man spins green chilies
over coals, dripping juice
that fills my head with heat,
my eyes with bristles.
Shutters hang crooked
over windows boarded up,
but fresh plaster stains a wall
beside a red gas pump.

I turn left again, pass honking geese,
pass chickens taking dust baths.
Turn right toward sunset.
I close the gate behind me
as if those bars could stop
the chill wind at my back,
the haze of cemetery dust.
I climb blue stairs
to a single bed and sleep.

At sunrise, a peculiar light
arranges on the window sill
blooms I cannot name.
I hang the hammock from the eaves.
Lie down to listen
as the tin roof cracks
in rhythm with the larks.
Great slow mountains lean
above the narrow valley.
I stare at slopes I've never walked.
Warm winds spin dust
to settle on my lips.

Today I taste familiar flavors
in unfamiliar earth. Today
I will begin to seek
my life without him. ೞ

The Wine Trees of Vallecitos

For Gina, Liz and those who knew Vallecitos

Walking uphill at dawn
I pass the empty church,
its clay floor swept each week.
A fresh mound crouches in the cemetery
near the first Christian buried here—
two centuries ago.
Weathered boards, face down,
tell nothing now.
Fading plastic flowers
tangle in tall grass.

At rest in a cedar
shaped like the ace of spades,
I wonder at the forms nature fashions
without thought or profit.
Each tree stands apart from every other,
recognizing in each root
that space is cushion,
distance a shield.

Against my back grows
a trunk thick as my thigh,
older than the Constitution.
Its curved boughs catch rain,
cradle my rump and shoulders.
Hidden here, I guard the trail.
Something glitters.
I unearth a wine bottle stained blue
by sunlight sifting through cedar boughs.
Burrowing, I find more flasks,
leaning together like old friends.

I imagine the village men
gathered here on downhill afternoons,
to drink and gossip in the pine tree's arms;
to detach themselves
from cutting hay or firewood;
to breathe in sanctuary.

Perhaps they saluted their little valley
from this wine tabernacle.
Perhaps they only drank,
grew old, died. Perhaps they lie
beneath those empty boards, these trees,
cradling in their dust
more empty bottles,
their salvation
and the trees' glass fruit. ᔕ

My Mother's Thumb

The kitchen sink is full of battered apples, squirrel-gnawed and robin-pecked.
I hack away the scars and salvage bits of fruit. At least I didn't
pick up windfalls as my mother always did. She said, "I can't
let them go to waste," forcing me to take a sack full. Hours
later, she'd be standing at the sink, nibbling bits of pith
off every core she'd gleaned. If I threw the apples to the chickens,
I'd know myself a double sinner, wasting time as well as food.
Today I see my mother's thumb, split and bleeding, braced against
my knife blade. While I peel these little nubbins, mother's in the nursing
home, smoothing lotion on her cracked, split fingertips.
I twist the paring knife, dig out a worm hole, leave the apple corer
on the pantry shelf because she taught me that a knife would waste less fruit.
When I stop to put a bandage on this thumb of hers, stained brown,
I see the clock and know at this time she'll be walking down the hall,
leaning on her wheelchair, singing to the aide about the surrey
with the fringe on top. She knows, they tell me, all the words, knows
addresses from apartments where she lived some sixty years ago.
When I present this apple pie to guests tonight, I'll tell them how
I made it from the damaged fruit, tell them that the recipe
was Mother's. I won't mention how we used to fight, or that she can't
recall my birthday, or this recipe. Last week she told me that
the saplings by her window at the nursing home won't bear
an apple for at least five years. ശ

The Poet Contemplates a Night Heron

For Jeff Crandall: brilliant poet, tough audience

She stands on granite dark as blood
at water's edge. Her reedy legs look fragile.
Her toes are locked to cloven rock,
to chips of mountain dropped here when the Rockies
fell. She settles, finds her balance. Stills. Her neck extends,
brown and white unraveling in the sun like snake skin.
She seems a painted bird of prey
in graceful watercolor, thin as mist upon her page,
her narrow beak a sharpened barb
above the pond. She waits
as spears of sunlight
pass the plane of day, dive beneath
the fluid's silky riffles, illuminate
a certain shape in every swell of wave.

Each day I watch her while I walk
the dogs around the lake, study
how she eyes the water, never seeming
to notice honking cars, the ducks and yappy dogs,
the children throwing bread and stones.

At last the slender beak descends,
a sudden hammer on a silver spine.
She flings her head back, tossing diamond droplets
high, engulfs the minnow in the long
dark throat of doom and swallows.
I picture silvery scales gliding down
the twists of gut. She stands erect, extends her wings
and leaves rock and water,
leaps into the air. Sunlight lures her up
beyond the water into the wider world
she's known, awash with flashing shapes
as sleek as moonlight's shaft. She's broken through
the barricade that seals the earth away
from sky and water. At last, I'm ready. ☙

The Empty Highway, The Unwritten Poem

For Mary Ellwein Spencer, who died December 28, 1966

Another day, another job: a talk
for high school students
and speech instructors in my home state.
Before I headed to your town, Mary,
you whispered in my ear all night.
Still, when I turned a hallway corner
and met your younger sister
I dropped a book. My brain lurched,
reversed, and spun back thirty years.
A thoughtful woman, she knows
how much she looks
the way you did the day you died.
She contrived to pat my arm —
she couldn't help herself—
and said, "If you still grieve for Mary
you should see a counselor,
get help from a professional."

All that day I thought I heard your laugh,
caught just a glimpse
as you went through a doorway.
Finally, you sat down beside me
for the final contest. A slender girl
announced she would interpret
Juliet's dialogue with her nurse
from *Romeo and Juliet.* In sympathetic silence
we each held our breath. She was
perfection as a love-struck teen
but hardly tired enough to be the nurse.
We who were the same at her age
nodded at each other and managed
not to giggle when she finished.

Had you really joined me that day,
your long fingers clothed in flesh,
we'd have hugged each other hard,
weaving again the strands of old affection.
We'd neither mention
graying hair or thickened waists.
You'd ask about my poems,
proclaim your grandchild's grades.
Naturally you'd have a grand*daughter!*
I'd apologize for writing so few letters,
ask if you'd stopped smoking.
Your short, sharp laugh
might crack into a cough
as you stretched a long arm
to flick ash aside
the way you did that last day.

There is no awkwardness,
no space between us.
You really haven't changed.
You've never gotten fat
or been betrayed. Love glows
in your eyes today
as in that bright December
thirty years ago.
The day you died beside your husband,
cradling the baby in your womb,
I made a vow: I'd never drive
that road again. Counseling myself,
I kept that vow until today.

The highway's wider now,
with warning signs on curves.
A tidy *x* keeps score of every death.
On highways by the dozen just like this one,
I've passed a thousand spots where other people
as beloved as you were died,
demolished by a lapse in care or too much speed.
Spun out on ice, or differed with some drunk.
I never knew their names. Rain washed
their blood from asphalt. Broken glass
crushed down to powder,
disappeared the way those tumbled leaves
scatter before my whirling tires.
For the pain you didn't suffer,
as well as all the joy you missed,
I finally cried today.

Raven lady, you were wise at twenty,
a sage among our flock of cackling poults
too busy preening fluff to think of death.
You were sisterhood to me,
as true as if we'd shared a home
and blood. Free with sound advice,
generous with love. Your slim hands
eased the pain between my shoulder blades
from bending to my books.
Later, I used my image of your smile
and acid tongue to shrivel nightmares—
some fanciful, some flesh.

So long ago, I thought I could avoid
the hurt with pure and simple detours.
Anyway, I always drive as if a demon
steers the oncoming car,
as if I might avoid his deadly aim
or choose a route not outlined on his map.
Your death was just the first
in a list too long to contemplate today.
I have no sister, but the stranger Death
has married into my family,
his face familiar as my own.
He comes to the reunion picnics,
pushes to the front in all the pictures.

Above me, geese announce their exit,
scribbling a momentary message
to those who drive this road,
to every farmer, framed inside
the box he calls a shelter belt.
This river valley where you died
is full of autumn odors
rising from the throbbing earth
to gravely touch my nostrils.
Leaves bright with life reel dying
in each auto's gusty wake. Low stones
crouching in a Mennonite burial ground
claim to represent forever.
A plain cross rises from a modest church.
The symbols are all here.

The thought of death would not
have kept you from any road
for thirty years. Riding at my side today,
you smile at souvenirs of memory,
sure the risks are worth the gamble. ∽

Loving the Cabinetmaker

For Jerry, again

You say, "I love you
but I'm not in love."
You're right, of course;
I love a man whose body
is becoming clay on a bare hill.
I can love you, if I choose.

Love is all that counts.
Politicians lie; governments steal.
Ministers fornicate with flocks,
God speaks in parables
and His interpreters cannot be trusted.
Love is all that stays
to stake our lives on.

I'd have bet my next breath
on that buried man,
believed my love
could save him.
Love's not for saving
but to spend.
Without his love,
I'm empty and alone.
So are you,
without hers.

Your hands fashion tables,
cabinets, stained-glass windows
as if you could
build love or beauty.
I write.
Loving does me nearly
as much good as being loved.
I want more
than a padded box
for cracked trinkets,
a closet full of memories,

Help me glue these remnants,
nail these blocks of scrap
into a graceful cupboard.
Let's trust
the straight-grained splice,
between us build
a treasure chest,
and fill it. ☙

Rhubarb Pie

Fifty finds me
a childless widow
with a new man.
Alone in my city garden
I pull rhubarb, grasping red stalks
down low, snapping them
from the girdle of ruffled leaves
the way grandmother taught me.
(We'd bend over crisp clusters of rhubarb
holding our breath
downwind from the skunk
she killed and buried with her hoe.)
Now I harvest this pie plant
for the bliss of sitting in deep grass,
slicing leaves off stalks
long as my forearm.
Cold water flushes away the dirt,
chills my wrists. Once
I dreamed a daughter
learning through me
the womanly rhythms of such work.

My grandmother married at sixteen,
at twenty-three became a widow with two babies.
Four years later, she married again,
bore her second husband two sons.
She was forty-five the day
he fell beside her on the hay cart,
dead with only time to say,

"I've done too much, Cora."
She raised her family on the canyon ranch,
gave her log house to the only one who stayed,
and moved into the bunkhouse. I always
slept snugly on her lumpy couch
below the screened porch windows.

In my city kitchen, I chop rhubarb stalks
that stain my fingers brown as the faded ink
of her pie recipe. I mix the honey
with orange rind, grated,
roll the flaky dough out thin as parchment.
Tonight, with my new man, I'll eat
this rhubarb pie at grandmother's old oak table,
thinking of the line of mothers, daughters
flowing back through time the way
lemon oil soaks into this dry wood.

Outside the window, dusk will hang
like smoke. Looking up, I'll see a child
reaching up to hold a wrinkled hand.
For the final time, I'll watch my daughter—
never conceived, never born, never named—
walk into the darkness with my grandmother. ∽

Pesto, On the Anniversary of Your Death

Eight years ago today I watched your coffin
lowered into gumbo on a prairie hill.
We banked the plain pine box with asters,
sunflowers, gayfeather twined in thistles.
Egyptian women scatter basil flowers
on the tombs of loved ones.
In Persia and Malaysia, women plant
basil on graves. I scattered coneflower,
sage and penstemon on yours.
Wild irises shelter you in May.

Today I kneel in blooms
I took from that plains hill
and planted here, beside a busy street.
I clip basil leaves with my fingernails.
Eight years ago, I chewed these nails
so short my fingers bled.
The Greeks believed that basil
would not grow without torment.
Planting its seeds, they shouted insults.
I push aside bee balm
and coriander to find parsley.
A leaf of basil on a Hindu's breast
becomes his passport to paradise.

Eight years ago, I'd never heard of pesto.
Back in my kitchen, loud with city sounds,
I pack basil leaves to fill a cup,
crushing leaves for the joy
of scent, snip them into slivers.
Jerry dices parsley while I chop
cloves of garlic, double what the recipe suggests.
His fist locked on my grandmother's grater,
he minces cheese — Parmesan, Romano —
into fluffy mounds. I rock the chopper over walnuts,
put everything into the blender.

Now's the time for patience. Gently
I tip the olive oil bottle,
watch the golden drizzle,
inhale the rising perfumes.
Slow grinding — a good technique for any job —
makes a pesto great,
like marriage or a friendship.

Tonight, we'll savor pesto over pasta,
remember you with laughter falling sometimes into silence.
Pesto can lie fresh for months
within its bed of olive oil.
I'll fill a spoon in January,
taste a summer past while winter hammers on the door,
loose a harvest fragrance
to mingle with the bitter hint of loss.
Tonight I'll laugh full-hearted in the candle glow,
loving you no less. Like me,
my new love knows the dark as well as light.
In Italy a man may love a maid
who gives him basil.
In Crete, basil is love
washed with tears. ~

Birthday Presents

So far I've unwrapped sunrise
from twenty thousand days.
At my birth, curls of ribbon fell
among starfish on a crystal beach
at Galveston. The gifts
of every age since then
take me farther from that sea.

I yanked especially sticky tape
from a lush sunrise in Iowa
and noticed that the sun
between straight rows of corn
cast a toxic greenish light.

A tangled skein of gold may still
lie hidden along a dirt road outside
Columbia, Missouri. Broken glass
and scraps of foil glint from a crevice
on a ridge where clouds
drop low. We tossed
strawberry leaves away,
left sugar crystals
dissolving in the rain
beside our wedding vows.

In a tipi under pines, I opened days
wrapped in a tanned deerhide
and tied with smoke. Cedar trunks
held beaver fur that flowed like water,
glass beads to plant among the lupine.
Each night, a grizzly bear
spun rocks the size of cars,
and still the sun rose sweet.

Together you and I untied one day
tethered with a mountain lion's tail.
She slipped through willow shade
to climb a sunny cliff
on an afternoon of strawberry-picking.
In Wyoming's razored mountains,
sky divers flew from cliffs of courage
floating down and safely far away.

I lifted foggy padding
from a valley deep in Wales,
walked by two gray horses,
saw the ribbons of the sun
stream out along my track.
I returned to find you sitting
among the pillows of our bed, sipping tea,
trying to curl your little finger
to make the proper mood.

Silver notes resounded from
the sunrise sack that held the banjo man.
His music lifted in the wind
to whirl around my ears—
and rings there still.

We ate blackberries
where Guinevere and Arthur once held court,
watched a silver jet scream overhead.
Later we were introduced
to twenty-four dun Jersey cows
pacing toward the barn, name tags
hanging in their ears.

The scraps of all those wrappings
lie beneath a rearing rock
crowned with eagle feathers,
wreathed in sage and sweetgrass prayers.

At times I've rummaged through the packing,
sure to find more tiny treasures,
friendships hidden in the corners,
men who stood between me and the dark,
women who kept their chins up,
dogs and even cats
who forgave me for their deaths.

Thick clouds over Greenland
hid the sunrise when our great plane
landed in its glow. Two friends drove off
to see the lochs we'd sung about for years.
That night, I understood how good
a man sat there beside me,
eating pea soup, crusty bread
before a fire of peat. At dawn
we walked the beach together,
holding hands.

So far, I've unwrapped a sunrise
from twenty thousand days or so.
I never stop to fold
and save the paper,
hoard the ribbon. ☙

Jigsaw Dance

For Jerry

All evening your saw growls
in the basement workshop as you build
a table with legs that dance.
I'm reading, slumped before the TV news,
when you come upstairs. Brushing
your teeth, you wander to the living room
to eye the two caged parrots
pictured on the lid of a puzzle box.
When you dump five hundred pieces,
I drop my book.

Together, bumping elbows gently
we turn them all face up.
I duck under your arm,
your hip grazes mine.
We sort out edges, corners,
show each other parts
we can identify.

I pull a chair close,
seize a cardboard corner,
build an edge—
a limit for the space we'll fill.
Your sleeve sweeps three pieces
to the floor. I pick them up,
find the eye you're missing.
You've moved the shape I need.
Biting my lip, I bend to seek it.
Silence. Breath. Bodies brushing.
Fit. Match what corresponds.

I walk away,
rinse dinner plates;
return to tuck a beak in place,
then put the lid on the butter dish.
You stare at jumbled pieces,
ponder, swear until you make
the right connection.
I sit. You stand.

When I lean back, the segment
in my hand fuzzes through my bifocals.
"You're in my light," you snap,
smartly tapping in a piece.
"Sorry. I'm shuffling identical
orange feathers." "I'm doing the black
background; that's harder."

When the real parrot shrieks
from his cage, I jump.
My knee jolts the table
scattering cardboard bits.
You pick them up, hand me
the one I need.

We move into each other's light
and out, circle the table,
build an image matching what we see.
We juggle fractured pieces,
try them left and right.
Sometimes your portion
of the picture overlaps my share.
When I present your missing claw,
your elbow jabs my ribs.

Eventually, we saunter down the hall,
arms interlocking,
climb into the same bed
and hold each other close. ဢ

BITTER CREEK JUNCTION

Benediction for Sweat

When you enter me,
I am black soil
rich with the humus
of ancestral bones
tilled smooth.

Breathing dust from your beard,
your hay-strewn hair,
I lick your skin
grateful for hard labor,
for all we plant
together, for sweat,
for the flavor of earth.

After Your Funeral

When I entered alone
the home we built together,
my footsteps echoed
from a black tombstone.
Stretching, I could scarcely
touch its crest.
Dumb, I traced your name.
Marble memorized
my fingerprints.

Crumpled in your chair,
I stared until sleep took me.
When morning light ricocheted
from window panes,
I took coffee to the deck.
There squatted an obsidian boulder.
While I sang your dawn prayer
it hummed discord.
I pushed against it,
sought for purchase
but the sides, scalpel sharp,
sliced my fingers.
Back in the kitchen,
our dining table wobbled
beneath a hollow stone,
dark mouth etched
with diamond teeth.

Three black stones.
One for each day without you.
Another stood above your grave.

In the company of stone,
I sorted papers, folded your clothes.
Each night I paced
while the rock on the deck
echoed each step.
When the phone rang,
the stone on the couch bonged.

Days passed. Slow nights
brought more black boulders.
I beat my fists against each one,
shattered the handle of a maul.
They neither moved nor broke.

Tumbling in our waterbed,
I dreamed of volcanoes,
of ashy clinkers grinding flesh.
Galena blocks on bookshelves
wept tears of lead.
Waxy opal globes
spun under my feet.

In daylight, I recalled
the hives of mason bees,
built of rock in streambeds,
hallways blocked with pebbles.
Caddisfly larvae fuse gravel chips
into armor before they crawl upstream.
I envisioned Mecca
where the faithful thousands march
begging mercy
around one black stone.

Each morning now I swerve
without a glance
around another.
Each grave guest
is harder than the last,
colder than your white flesh
on clean hospital sheets
that last midnight.
"Marry again," you said,
but even if I do,
I won't come home
to find the stones are gone.
I am
accustomed to them. ෴

Reading in Bed

Neither of us ever did,
saving the bed for sleep or love.
Still, we lived half our waking lives
in words on paper. On days
when our harmony was too frail
for speech, we concealed ourselves
inside our heads.
I wrote. You read.

Now I realize that during
that last summer of your life,
I seldom saw you sleep.
The cancer in your spine
made lying down too painful.
Instead you napped upright
in your chair, a book beside you.

From ragged sleep I'd wake
to light from the living room,
your husky breathing.
I'd kneel beside you,
hold your hand,
smooth the blanket
over your shoulders.
You were always awake
staring at the eastern windows
blank with darkness.
You'd stroke my hair,
send me back to bed.
In the morning I'd bring coffee,
find your eyes closed,
breath hushed,
face so still I'd gasp,
shove the thought of death away.

Now I spend long evenings
in your chair, pretend to read
until the dog goes to the bedroom,
winds himself around
your pillow into sleep.
Facing those windows,
I watch for whatever held your gaze.

Each morning when I wake
as light spills
in the windows from the east,
you are still gone.
Today it's been three months.
Elsewhere, dreamers
survived again Pearl Harbor,
awakened screaming.
I dreamed you
sitting in your easy chair
smiling as you faced the dark. ☙

Deathbed Gift

"Watch the sunsets," you said,
instead of the last goodbye.
That first New Year's Day,
I resolved to watch them all.
(Do you see sunsets
from inside that glow?)

The first night, light
flamed red-gold across
the black hills.
On the third night,
massed clouds blushed.
The twelfth was blue.
Standing in thigh-deep snow
I warmed my hands
on my own heart.

Burning forests made
two-hundred-seventy-one
black and red. Hot ash singed my hair.
Sunset three-hundred-fifty dimmed
while I shivered and planted
iris bulbs on your grave.

By the third year, I'd missed a few,
caught inside a building,
head bent to a book.
But I always heard your words.
On the third anniversary
of the day you died,
a man leaned on your tombstone
crying for you. He said to me,
"Give yourself sunsets."

Sunset begins tonight
in shades of pink and gold.
On the north horizon,
long tatters curl eastward
like discarded ribbons. ☙

Widow's Homemade Sachet

Flowers from the girls' dresses,
stripes from my son's pajamas,
denim from my husband's shirts,
worn soft—I spent autumn evenings
sewing these scraps into pouches
the size of my palm.
At twilight of some autumn day
when sun trickled weakly
through forest fire haze
and cold flowed around my ankles,
I knelt in the garden snipping
bay, spearmint, sage and thyme.

I carried baskets of herbs
to the food dryer, piled up
lavender, oregano, parsley.
Each time I passed that way
I breathed bouquets like liquor.
When the first snow glided down,
I filled each little bag
with the scent of solstice.

Tonight, with winter coming,
I hear the dog bay as the moon rises.
The only lavender I can find
hangs in the sunset on the hills.
I don't have time for tiny stitches.
Diligent, I weed the balance sheet,
till a loan, cultivate the mortgage.
I can't mint money, so I must
let the fences lean.
I've harvested the crop of debt
my father sowed. Now
I'll harrow his memory smooth,
shovel manure to my creditors.

Sleepless, I resolve to make
one last sachet just for myself.
I cut a rough patch
from long underwear softened against
my husband's stubborn hide.
Gathering fabric on my needle,
I find time to wonder if my dead father
still fights my dead husband.
On cemetery hill, they've settled
on estates so small there's barely room
for me between them.
I stuff the sack with herbs,
tie a careful bow with ribbon
from my basket of discarded scraps.

After midnight, while the dog snores
on my husband's pillow,
I ease the dresser drawer open,
slip the bag inside
to sleep while the earth turns,
until I know if the years and cash
I've planted here will be enough
to pay the taxes,
to keep this land
scented with my father's blood,
my husband's sweat, my love. ☙

Café Sleep

I close my eyes,
opening them on the other side
where I sink into a padded booth
opposite my husband, dead
now but always waiting.
It's happy hour at Café Sleep.
Fear lies across an amber riffle
in his mug of beer. Laughter
blends our separated lives
like the scotch in my glass.
We talk of old friends, lovers,
murmur memories. We consider
time steeped in sunsets,
rivers always running west.

Some nights we leave the smoky pub
to stroll foggy streets,
enter a familiar house
through a warped door
left open for us.
We sit on dusty cushions
admiring woodwork burnished
by our own hands, recall photos
we placed on these walls
in frames now empty. Near dawn,
we rest on the floor
of an unroofed room.

When I wake, I am alone,
my husband's face
a sunlight-faded photograph.
I've forgotten
every story we told,
all the names. ☙

How Women Laugh In the Company of Men

We never shout, never belly a laugh
like those gushing down dormitory halls
behind jokes you couldn't tell your mother.
Never guffaw open-mouthed.
Never roar until our sides ache and tears flow.
Dining with a man, we never
squirt milk out our noses.
Never never laugh so hard we fart.

In the company of men we chuckle.
He's not sure? Buoyant laughter.
Can't commit? *Ha ha* laughs a girl
with time and choices. He jokes?
Giggle behind a hand, hiding your teeth,
a maiden to be protected. When your boss
tells you in confidence he hopes
you're not one of those liberated women
just looking for a sexual harassment case,
smile sweetly past the gurgle in your throat.

In the high school staff lounge,
the handsome football coach reports
what the dumb blonde said to the pilot.
Every woman chortles, even the one
so liberated she took her mother's name.
The bitter widow titters. A chemistry teacher
snickers through a doughnut.
She's outlived three husbands,
buried several hundred students,
many of them alive.

Ladylike laughter hisses
between painted lips in company lobbies,
echoes down every gas-chamber-green
hallway in the country.
A shy girl with acne
clutches her books like a shield,
giggling as the quarterback handles her.
Knowing how to time a laugh
eases a woman's way in commerce.
A woman in high heels and slit skirts
who knows when to laugh
can romp right up that corporate ladder.

Having trouble, ladies? Women skilled
at mirth in proper measure
teach comprehensive classes,
where models demonstrate laughing
through gritted teeth.
Advanced Laughter Seminars
meet late, behind drawn curtains,
in a basement room with no windows.
Masked women in black
tutor select students,
a squad of women
who have chosen
to stop laughing. ☙

Bitter Creek Junction

❖ Part One.

All cruelty springs from weakness.
—SENECA (4 B.C.–A.D. 65)

As usual, the shortcut proves
longer than the map promised.
I cross the railroad tracks
and nothing looks familiar anymore.
I dry my forehead on my sleeve.
Clench my jaw, teeth grinding grit.

How long has it been? Not long enough.
Two men in a beat-up white sedan
once followed me on the interstate.
They passed a dozen times, edging closer.
When I drove fast, hoping to flush out
a cop with radar, they kept pace,
easing ever nearer. For miles I looked
for a ranch house, gas station, any place
I might find help or haven. Side by side
we raced along the highway, doing eighty.
The fender of the white car
grazed mine as they passed again.

I'd had enough. The driver dropped back
beside me once more, smirking while
the other man whooped, "Pull over, honey!"
I laid the barrel of my pistol
flat across my steering arm
and watched his tires. One inch closer
and I'd pull the trigger. No need to aim.
The white car shot away. Years later
I grip the steering wheel,
remembering, my knuckles white.

White in all directions. I breathe
alkali dust and coast on downhill grades,
watch the needle on the gas gauge
riding empty one long mile, another.
Sunset flares before I see the interstate,
skylined eighteen-wheelers rolling west.

Rattling on a pole, a crumpled sign
announces, "Gas Bar" beside a fuel pump's
broken concrete base. I stand
in waist-high weeds to fill the tank.
Three beat-up pickups nose against the wall,
boxes full of chains and oily rags.
A skinny cat slumps at a corner.
I step through the open door and pause,
dazed by the dark inside, the smell
of beer gone flat, spoiled food.
The place is half groceries, half saloon.

"Git out of her way!"
A gaunt man shoulders me aside
to slap a toddling girl.
He grabs her arm, and shakes her
while her dark eyes reach for mine.
"Pay attention when I talk to you!"
He yanks her hair to make her face him.
"How much?" he says. Shoves the girl away.
"I'm talkin' to you, Blondie. How much gas?
I don't have no way to know that
from in here."

"Nine fifty-five," I say, and notice
the woman in the gloom behind the bar.
She sets beer before three men
who turn their heads to look at me.
Her long dark hair hangs straight,
not hiding bruises on her eyes and cheeks.
She takes the bill I give her,
hands me coins in change and never
once looks up. The child clings to her skirt.

At the bar, one man elbows another,
spins around to leer at me,
his legs spread wide. He grins
and scratches slowly. "Saturday night!"
one says. "Time to party!"
The jowly one points his bottle at me,
yelps, "Party enough for all of us right there."
I yank my cap low, getting ready
for the ceaseless prairie crosswinds.
I plant my feet and take the time
to squint and glare at every man.

Cans and bottles rattle in the back room.
The man yells, "Yer brat's been drinkin' pop again,
squaw. I'll tan her hide!" The three men laugh.
The child stands at my knee, looking up.
I dig for the ten in my pocket as I kneel.
"You're a good girl," I say, and slip
the folded bill into her grimy little hand.
Smoothly, she makes the money vanish
without a glance behind her.

I grip my car keys like a weapon
in my right hand, open the car door
with my left. I turn the ignition
while I shift, and the men inside stand up.
I spin the steering wheel and gun it,
clang gravel off the signs and pickup windows.

One tough woman howls a challenge
from my stereo. Roaring up the access road,
I drop between two trucks,
lock the needle at eighty-five.
I keep up with the convoy
while I watch for headlights
to follow me from Bitter Creek.

Bonnie Raitt joins me running west.
She rides shotgun, crooning songs
of freedom, blues about the men
who have abused and left us all,
and what we hope will happen to them.
While my car burns the costly fuel
from Bitter Creek, I sing so loud
I know I'm trying not to think,
don't want to guess how many times
she's been called a *squaw.*
I want to pray for that woman,
for the child, even for the man.
Sisters! Pray for the souls of the damned,
but teach your daughters to be brave.

As I drive a shaft of light
across that black and stony plain
I brood about the woman and her daughter,
I know some deer hunter
may one day stumble on their bones
scattered in an icy gulch.
I grind my teeth and dream revenge,
test the polished edge of rage against my fear.
I chase the sunset's light,
carve a path through shadows,
leaving tracks I hope that she will follow.

Part Two.

All oppression creates a state of war.
—SIMONE DE BEAUVOIR, *THE SECOND SEX,* 1949

Every year, up near Battle Mountain,
some bunch of hunters finds a heap of bones,
maybe a scrap of cloth, a warped boot sole.
Their cell phone declares it's too far out of range
for calls, so they look up a lawman when they get back to town.
The sheriff shrugs, hitching up his gun belt,
mumbling something about sheepherders
and the Blizzard of '49. Then he gets a call,
a tanker wrapped around a Winnebago
on the interstate. He'll check the bones,
sometime when he's out that way.
If they follow him outside, protesting,
he says patiently, "Don't worry about it, fellas.
We find a dozen of 'em a year. Basement's
full of boxes, bones somebody hauled in here
we'll never put a name to. Every ten years or so,
we bury 'em and start all over."

Part Three.

There's no question in my mind but that rights are never won unless people are willing to fight for them.
—ELEANOR SMEAL
SPEECH TO THE NATIONAL PRESS CLUB, 1985

A woman must be smart
to survive, must understand
when her time has come.
She can't take more abuse
than her daughter can stand.
Already the child's eyes are dim.

While she plans defection,
a cunning woman will pretend servility,
ignore the snickers,
endure the men who prod and pinch
with eyes and fingers.
When he slaps her while they watch
she won't grab the scattergun under the bar.
She'll scurry. Bend. Think.
Not yet. Not yet.
Still, in a land of drunken homesteads,
dead-end roads and desert dust,
a woman often learns
she has to help herself.

She might spread old blankets
over the couch, cast them wide and thick.
When he staggers toward their bed,
she could tell him it's her time of month,
wave him toward the other room.
Steady and sober, she'll tuck
the child in early, close the door.
Then wait. Wait until he snores.

She might ease from the covers,
slide her feet over the floor
to keep the loose board quiet.
Put on a pair of his gloves.
Take the big moss agate from the shelf.
Tie a towel around it.
Make knots to fit her hands.
Swing the weight to test
its mass against her arm.
Standing by the couch she'll breathe
deeply of his sweat and smoke.
Steady herself. Swing.
Strike between the eyes.
More than once. Then stop.

Push his stench out of her lungs and
listen for his breath. She won't
take time to sob or stare.
She'll drop the rock beside his head.
Wrap the blankets tight.
Without a light, she'll drag him to the pickup.
Drop the tailgate, haul him up.
Cover him with his own tarp,
still bloody from the last poached deer.
Be sure she has the shovel he used
to bury the guts.
Gloves still on, headlights off,
she'll pick a dirt road
pounded every day by a hundred pickups
headed for an oil field or a trona mine.
She knows the roads.

She'll drive deep into the desert,
come home before the day dawns red,
nothing but a shovel rattling
in the truck's bed. Park his truck
the way a drunk would leave it,
sleep sound beside her child.
At daylight she'll inspect the couch,
the ground around the door,
the pickup box. If she sees blood,
she won't wash it out—he wouldn't.
Maybe she'll do as he did every fall,
shoot a dozen of the starving cats,
throw them in the pickup box
to swell and stink until she hauls
the weekly trash out to the rubbish pile.

If anyone asks about the man,
she'll stay in her familiar shadow.
Shrug. Say little. She didn't notice.
She closed the bar, went to bed
as usual. He was drinking
with some woman, some drillers,
roughnecks she never saw before.
Didn't come to bed. That's all she knows.
She won't mention the bruises.
They've all been here to drink
when he was slapping her around.
She'll run the bar the way she always did,
add the money to her hideout cash.
Stay out of trouble. Maybe move
next summer. Find some place
where she can walk in sunshine
with her daughter,
humming an old blues tune. ∽

—Written for the battered woman
at the place I call Bitter Creek for her protection

ACKNOWLEDGMENTS

All poems have been revised since they first appeared in earlier publications.

"Benediction for Sweat": An early version was published in *InterMountain WOMAN,* July 1997, Vol. 1, No. 6, p. 15.

"Death of the Last Cowhand": Years ago, a friend sent me a clipping about Tom Blasingame's death from the obituary column of the *Albany* (New York) *Times Union* dated December 31, 1989. His attached note said, "Isn't there a great L.H. poem in this?" Thanks, Hobie, and sorry it took me so long to write.

"How Women Laugh in the Company of Men": Earlier published as "How Women Laugh When They're With Men," in *The Temple,* Vol. 1 #2, 1997, p. 52–3.

"International Incident": Published in an earlier version in *Prairie Schooner,* Spring 1993.

"Rhubarb Pie": First published in *Red Weather,* student, alumni and faculty (including visiting writers) magazine, Moorhead State University, Moorhead, MN, Spring 1998, No. 17, p. 49.

"The Wine Trees of Vallecitos": Performance, included in taped highlights of 1997 Cowboy Poetry Gathering, distributed by the Western Folklife Center, Elko, Nevada. First published in *Water-Stone,* journal of the graduate liberal studies program, Hamline University, St. Paul, Minnesota, Vol. I, No, 1, Fall, 1998, pp. 206–207.

Linda M. Hasselstrom divides her time between her ranch in South Dakota and her home in Wyoming.

She is the author of three previous volumes of poetry and six non-fiction books, and has been a featured performer at the National Cowboy Poetry Gathering in Elko and the People's Poetry Gathering in New York City. With Gaydell Collier and Nancy Curtis, she co-edited *Leaning into the Wind*, an anthology of writing by plains women, selected as one of nineteen outstanding nonfiction books of the year by the *Christian Science Monitor.*

Hasselstrom operates a writing retreat for women, Windbreak House, on the family ranch where she lived and worked for over forty years. After years as an activist, Hasselstrom now believes she can work most effectively to preserve her plains homeland by writing.

She has presented hundreds of workshops, holds an M.A. in American Literature, and has taught in various colleges. She formerly directed both an independent publishing house and a literary magazine.

The text is twelve-point Garamond
by Adobe.
Display type is Skylark ITC and
RoadWarningSigns by Benn Coifman.
The book is printed on
sixty-pound Glatfelter Supple Opaque Natural,
a recycled, acid-free paper,
by Thomson Shore.